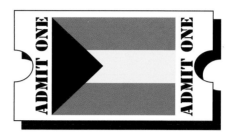

Snorkeler And Pillar Coral

FACES
AND
PLACES

# THE BAHAMAS

BY BOB TEMPLE

THE CHILD'S WORLD ®

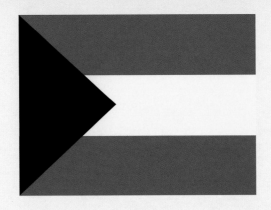

## COVER PHOTO

A smiling student in Inagua.
©Bob Krist/CORBIS

**Published in the United States of America by The Child's World®**
PO Box 326
Chanhassen, MN 55317-0326
800-599-READ
www.childsworld.com

**Project Manager** James R. Rothaus/James R. Rothaus & Associates
**Designer** Robert E. Bonaker/R. E. Bonaker & Associates
**Contributors** Mary Berendes, Dawn M. Dionne, Katherine Stevenson, Ph.D., Red Line Editorial

The Child's World® and Faces and Places are the sole property
and registered trademarks of The Child's World®.

**Library of Congress Cataloging-in-Publication Data**
Temple, Bob.
The Bahamas / by Bob Temple.
p. cm.
Includes index.
ISBN 1-56766-904-2 (lib. bdg. : alk. paper)
1. Bahamas—Juvenile literature. [1. Bahamas.] I. Title.
F1651.2 .T46 2003
972.96—dc21
00-013182

Table of Contents

If you looked down on Earth from above, you would see **continents**, large land areas surrounded by oceans. Earth also has many small islands of land that would be harder to see. The Bahamas are a group of islands in the Caribbean Sea, near the continent of North America.

*Western Hemisphere*

*Eastern Hemisphere*

Both The Bahamas (white) and U.S.A. (green) are in the west

The Bahamas include about 700 small islands. The northernmost islands are just southeast of the state of Florida.

The southernmost are near the island nation of Cuba. Andros, the Bahamas' largest island, is about 104 miles long and 40 miles wide.

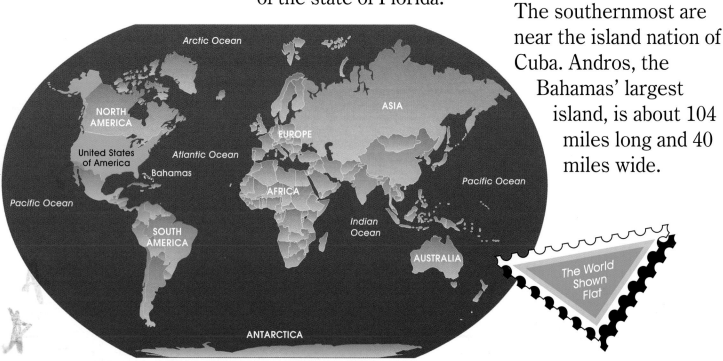

The World Shown Flat

UNITED STATES
*(FLORIDA)*

*Atlantic Ocean*

BAHAMAS

*Caribbean Sea*

CUBA

HAITI   DOMINICAN
REPUBLIC

JAMAICA

Islands
In The
Bahamas

Nassau
Andros Island
Stocking Island
Cat Island
Mount Alvernia

Boats On The Shore Of Stocking Island

**A**ll the islands in the Bahamas are very flat. The highest point in the country, Mount Alvernia, is a hill that rises only 206 feet above the level of the surrounding sea. The Bahamas' flat landscape isn't boring, however—there are miles and miles of warm, sandy beaches!

The Port Of Nassau

The Bahamas have only two seasons: summer and winter. Summer lasts from May to November, and winter lasts from December to April. Winters are only about 11 degrees cooler than summers—much less of a difference than in many parts of the world! Summers carry the threat of occasional **hurricanes**, storms with damaging winds and heavy rains.

ADMIT ONE  ADMIT ONE

A Flock Of Flamingos

The Bahamas have a warm, moist, **tropical** climate. Many types of plants and animals thrive in this tropical weather. Beautiful flowers such as orchids and jasmine grow throughout the islands. There are also palm trees, cork trees, olive trees, and some thicker forests.

©Richard Hamilton Smith/CORBIS

Bluestriped Grunts Swimming Around A Shipwreck

©Stuart Westmorland/CORBIS

The Bahamas are home to many types of birds, including a large number of flamingos, the islands' national bird. Inagua National Park has more than 50,000 flamingos—the largest flock in the world. Frogs, snakes, and lizards also call the Bahamas home. Colorful fish and other sea creatures swim in the coral reefs off the coasts.

Eleuthera Island
●Governor's Harbour

Inagua National
Park ── ●Great Inagua
Island

Long Seed Pods On A Poinciana Tree In Governor's Harbour

Nassau

San Salvador

©CORBIS

Columbus
Lands On
San Salvador
In 1492

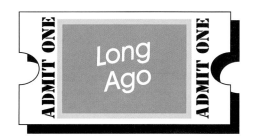

The Bahamas were once home to the Lucayan, a group of Arawak Indians who came from South America. These peaceful people survived by fishing. In 1492, Christopher Columbus sailed from Spain and reached the islands.

The Spanish rounded up the Lucayan people and took them to America to be slaves. Because of this, the Bahamas were **uninhabited**, or empty, when the British later arrived and took control. The British ruled the Bahamas as a **colony** starting in 1670.

The land of the Bahamas has never been very good for farming, and the Bahamian people remained poor. After World War II, Americans began to see the Bahamas as a nice vacation spot. Sandy beaches, beautiful blue water, and warm weather brought lots of people—and their money. This new **tourist** trade helped make the Bahamas more successful.

Ruins Of A French Building In Nassau

©Dave G. Houser/CORBIS

# The Bahamas Today

A Resort On Paradise Island

The Bahamas remained under British rule for over two centuries. In 1967, Bahamian people formed the Progressive Liberal Party, which worked to bring independence to the Bahamas. The Bahamas finally became an independent nation on July 10, 1973.

©David Allen/CORBIS

Parliament Building In Nassau

©Mark Gibson/CORBIS

Today, the Progressive Liberal Party is still in power. The British still appoint a governor-general for the Bahamas, but that person has little power. Instead the nation is run by a prime minister and the elected leaders in the House of Assembly, a **legislature** similar to the United States Congress. The Bahamas is better off financially than it used to be, thanks mostly to tourism.

©Dave G. Houser/CORBIS

Paradise Island
Nassau

Matthew Town • Great Inagua

Children In
Nassau

Nassau

Great Exuma

The Bahamas is a mixture of European and African cultures. About 80 percent of the people are black. Almost all of the people are of the Christian faith, with about one-third of them being Baptist. About one-fifth of the people are Roman Catholic.

Years ago, many of the black people of the Bahamas were slaves. In 1834, slavery was outlawed, but black people still were not given the same rights as white people. Racism, the belief that some people are better than others because of the color of their skin, was a big problem.

Since 80 percent of the people of the Bahamas are black, they felt that they should be represented in the country's government. Even during this time, however, the people of the Bahamas got along. Since the Progressive Liberal Party gained power, things have been more fair for all people in the Bahamas.

A House On North Bimini

Only about 40 of the Bahamas' 700 islands are inhabited. During the 1970s, many people moved from smaller islands to the larger islands such as New Providence. Today, about two-thirds of the nation's people live in cities on these busier islands. The cities are usually right on the ocean and are popular tourist attractions.

An Outdoor Straw Market In Nassau

The smaller islands have fewer people and a more old-fashioned way of life. Some islands don't even have electricity. The people live off the land and the water, eating the food they can grow or the fish they can catch. When they need supplies, they must go to one of the larger islands. The Flying Doctor Service brings doctors by airplane to care for the sick or injured.

©Tony Arruza/CORBIS

©Bob Krist/CORBIS

©James Davis; Eye Ubiquitous/CORBIS

Bimini

New Providence Island

Nassau

Dunmore Town

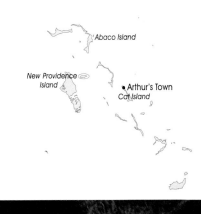

New Providence
Island

Abaco Island

Arthur's Town
Cat Island

A Girl
Attending
Class
In Arthur's
Town On
Cat Island

Almost everyone in the Bahamas can read and write. Bahamian children start school at age 5 and must stay in school until age 14. Most children stay in school longer. All students learn a musical instrument until the ninth grade.

Many people go on to college, but because there are no four-year colleges in the country, they must study elsewhere. Many students attend college in the United States.

Bahamas 700 Islands

NASSAU 113
WALKERS CAY 52
GREAT EXUMA 246
MIAMI 112
ELEUTHERA 171
MONTREAL 1,323
ANDROS 103
GREAT ABACO 50
NEW YORK 1,015
GREAT INAGUA 438

©Bob Krist/CORBIS

A Signpost On New Providence Island

A Teacher Helping Students On Abaco Island

©Catherine Karnow/CORBIS

English is the Bahamas' official language. Bahamian English sounds different from English spoken in other regions. When Bahamians speak English, it sounds almost as if they are singing rather than just talking!

A Sailboat Builder On Andros Island

©Dave G. Houser/CORBIS

About 40 percent of Bahamians work at resorts or other businesses that serve tourists. Most others work in other types of businesses. The Bahamian government does not charge taxes on businesses or on people's paychecks.

Many overseas businesses have offices in the Bahamas because they can keep more of the money they make. Bahamian cities house hundreds of banks from many different countries.

Farmers Harvesting Crops On Long Island

©Bob Krist/CORBIS

A small number of Bahamian people make their living farming or fishing. Because farming is not successful and the country is so small, the Bahamas must trade with other nations to get the supplies people need. The United States is the Bahamas' biggest trading partner.

Nassau

Andros Island

Long Island

Tourists
And Cruise Ships
In Nassau

Fantasy

FANTASY

A Man Cleaning Fish At A Market Near Nassau

Grand Bahama Island
Freeport

Bimini Islands

Nassau

©Stuart Westmorland/CORBIS

# Food

A Fruit Stand In Freeport On Grand Bahama Island

©Bob Krist/CORBIS

Seafood is plentiful in the Bahamas, thanks to the ocean waters that surround the islands. Crabmeat and fish are popular foods. Juicy tropical fruits also grow on the islands, including pineapples, bananas, grapefruits, and mangoes. There is little room on the islands to raise cattle and other animals, so red meat is not a common food.

Cooking Seafood Fritters On The Bimini Islands

©Tony Arruza/CORBIS

Traditional dishes include peas and rice, Bahamian lobster, stewed or boiled fish, seafood fritters, and fresh bread. Because of the large number of tourists that go to the Bahamas, you can also find lots of different kinds of restaurants. Chinese, Mexican, Creole, Indian, and Japanese food can all be found.

Bahamians love music and dancing. Talented musicians perform everywhere from opera houses to street corners. Both adults and children also enjoy a board game called *Warri*. Sports are popular, too—especially baseball, basketball, tennis, and track. Many Bahamians have been very successful in sports, either in the Olympic Games or as sports professionals in other countries.

Bahamian people celebrate many of the same holidays we do. They have a Labor Day and an Independence Day, although they fall on different days than they do in the U. S.

Bahamians celebrate the Christian holidays of Christmas and Easter, as well as Boxing Day (which falls on December 26). On Boxing Day and New Year's Day, they enjoy *Junkanoo* parades in which costumed dancers move through the streets to loud, fast-paced music.

The Bahamas is a very friendly place. The people are nice, and the weather and the sights are wonderful. If your family needs a nice, relaxing vacation, perhaps you should consider the Bahamas!

The Bahamas' Women's Relay Team After Winning A Gold Medal In The 2000 Olympics

©Reuters NewMedia Inc./CORBIS

West End
Freeport

Nassau

©Philip Gould/CORBIS

A Junkanoo
Parade In
Nassau

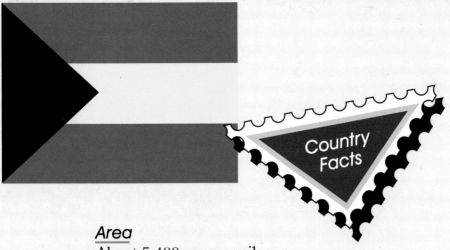

## Area
About 5,400 square miles
(14,000 square kilometers) spread over about 700 islands—a total area slightly smaller than the state of Connecticut.

## Population
About 293,000 people.

## Capital City
Nassau (on New Providence Island).

## Other Important Cities
Freeport, West End.

## Money
The Bahamian dollar, which is divided into 100 cents.

## National Flag
Two blue stripes on the top and bottom and a yellow stripe in the middle. The left side of the flag includes a black triangle. The two blue stripes stand for the beautiful water that surrounds the islands. The yellow stripe represents the Bahamas' sunny shores, and the black triangle is a symbol of the vigor and force of the people.

## National Song
"March on Bahamaland."

## Official Name
The Commonwealth of the Bahamas.

## Head of Government
The prime minister.

A Costumed Man In A Junkanoo Parade

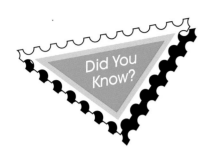

The oceans around the Bahamas are great for diving. Divers can swim near dolphins, look at sea turtles and thousands of colorful fish, and maybe even see a shark!

After the British took control of the Bahamas, they had trouble surviving off the land. So they turned to piracy, raiding passing ships and stealing the goods they needed.

Mychal Thompson, who grew up in the Bahamas, played professional basketball in the United States and won an NBA Championship as a member of the Los Angeles Lakers.

During Prohibition, from 1920 to 1933, alcohol was outlawed in the United States. "Bootleggers" who sold illegal liquor used the Bahamas for secretly transporting liquor.

|  | BAHAMIAN ENGLISH | HOW TO SAY IT |
| --- | --- | --- |
| Wow! | Mudasick! | moo–DAH–sick |
| "No doubt" or "for sure" | for true | FOR TROO |
| My friend | ma 'bwoy | ma–BOY |
| How are you? | All's well? | ALLZ WELL |
| Everything is okay. | All's well. | ALLZ WELL |
| Thing as in "Gimme that thing." | "Gimme that tingum." | TING–um |
| I'm tired. | I blow. | EYE BLOW |

**colony (KOL-uh-nee)**
A colony is a land that is ruled by a faraway country. England once ruled the Bahamas as a colony.

**continents (KON-tih-nents)**
A continent is a large area of land surrounded mostly by water. The Bahamas lie near the continent of North America.

**hurricanes (HUR-ih-kaynz)**
Hurricanes are damaging tropical storms with very strong winds and heavy rains. Hurricane season in the Bahamas runs from mid-July to mid-November.

**legislature (LEJ-iss-lay-tchur)**
A legislature is a group of elected leaders who make a nation's laws. The Bahamian legislature is called the House of Assembly.

**tourist (TOOR-ist)**
A tourist is someone who travels to another place to sightsee and visit. Many tourists visit the Bahamas, especially from the United States.

**tropical (TROP-ih-kull)**
Tropical places have warm, wet weather all year long. The Bahamas is a tropical country.

**uninhabited (un-in-HAB-ih-ted)**
If an area is uninhabited, it doesn't have any people living in it. When the British arrived in the Bahamas, the islands were uninhabited.

## Index

Web Sites

### Learn more about the Bahamas!

Visit our homepage for lots of links about the Bahamas:
**http://www.childsworld.com/links.html**

*Note to Parents, Teachers, and Librarians:*
We routinely verify our Web links to make sure they're safe,
active sites—so encourage your readers to check them out!